THE NEGRO WORKER

AN ADDRESS

delivered by

EUGENE VICTOR DEBS

On TUESDAY, OCTOBER 30, 1923

AT

COMMONWEALTH CASINO
135th Street and Madison Ave.,
New York City
Under the Auspices of the 21st A. D.
Socialist Party of
New York

WILDSIDE PRESS

Chairman

FRANK R. CROSSWAITH

Chairman, Committee of Arrangements

G. OLLENDORFF

Preliminary Speakers

JAMES ONEAL
Author "The Next Emancipation"

A. PHILLIP RANDOLPH
Editor "The Messenger"

LUCILLE RANDOLPH
Aldermanic Candidate 21st A. D.

HON. JUDGE JACOB PANKEN

INTRODUCTION

After the preliminary speeches by Comrades James Oneal, author of "The Next Emancipation"; A. Phillip Randolph, editor of "The Messenger," and Mrs. Lucille Randolph, the chairman of the meeting, Frank R. Crosswaith, presented Mr. Debs with the following glowing remarks:

"And now, comrades and friends, the moment that we have all so anxiously awaited is here. I know with what eagerness you yearn for the eloquent voice, the sweet and inspiring personality of this great man, and his great message. Here is a personality full of that precious tenderness so rare in the average individual, but so much in evidence with Eugene V. Debs. (Applause.)

"Seven years ago I joined the Socialist Party, little did I dream then that I would be the recipient of such an enviable honor as this: the honor of presenting this great character to an audience even though it be in this segregated section of New York City. I stand before you, friends, and say, in all boldness, that I am indeed proud of this honor, and equally proud to be a Socialist hailing this modern crusader as my comrade.

"I have read some history. I have read of such stalwart figures as John Brown, Frederik Douglass, Wendell Phillips, Elijah Lovejoy, Denmark Vessey, Sojourner Truth and others; I have followed with pride the record of their contributions to human progress, as told in the eloquent though mute pages of history. But in reading of these great benefactors, one thing impresses me most of all, and that is, that during their lifetime these brave men and women were despised by society—society ridiculed them, persecuted them, even lynched some of them; then, after they were dead, after their eyes had been closed by the remorseless hand of death, after Mother Earth had opened wide her unprejudiced arms and pressed their lifeless limbs close to her maternal bosom, it was then only that the world recognized their greatness and built monuments to them. In other words, these historic characters came into their own only after they were dead and then garlands were woven for their graves. This, my friends, has been the conduct of the blind majority in every age toward the far-sighted few.

"But here is one whose greatness the world is now beginning audibly to acknowledge, before death shall have silenced his song-seeped soul. Here is a man that is loved, honored and revered in every section of the civilized world where the brutal hands of capitalism and tyranny rule and where the common people hunger for liberty and life. Yes, wherever men thirst for the cooling waters of knowledge and freedom, the name of Eugene V. Debs is known. (Prolonged applause.)

"Tempted as I am on this historic occasion to make a speech, I will, nevertheless, resist the temptation by presenting to you Freedom's most fearless fighter, oppression's most valiant foe, Labor's most eloquent and loyal champion, the Negro's true friend—Comrade Eugene V. Debs." (Thunderous and prolonged applause.)

Appeal to Negro Workers

by

EUGENE V. DEBS

Tuesday Evening, October 30, 1923

Mr. Debs: Friends and Comrades and Fellow-workers—I feel especially complimented by the invitation which has made it possible for me to stand in this inspiring presence to-night. I must first of all thank you and each of you in all sincerity for this very cordial greeting—this hearty manifestation of your sympathy and goodwill for the cause for which I am to speak to you to-night, and for the all too generous introduction of my young Comrade, the Chairman of the occasion, which touches me too deeply for words. I return my thanks to the dear little children whose floral offerings so enrich and reward me for the little that I have been able to do in the service of this great cause. The one regret of my life is that I have so little to give in return for all that is given me.

This great movement which I have been trying to serve; this movement in the interest of a higher social order, a nobler humanity, a diviner civilization that has given me my principles and my ideals and the right to live and to serve—I am only sorry that it is in my power to give so little in return.

I am more than glad to see the colored people represented here to-night. From the beginning of my life my heart has been with them. I never could understand 6why they were denied any right or any privilege or liberty that the white man

5

had a right to enjoy. I never knew of any distinction on account of the color of the flesh of a human being. Indeed, when
I think of what the colored people have been made to suffer
at the hands of their supposedly superior race, every time I
look a colored brother in the face I blush for the crimes that
my race has committed against his race. (Great applause.)

I do not speak to my colored friends to-night in any patro-
nising sense; I meet them upon a common basis of equality;
they are my brothers and my sisters, and I want nothing that
is denied them, and if there is one of them who will shine my
shoes and I am not willing to shine his, he is my moral superior. (Applause.) One reason why I became a Socialist was
because I was opposed to this cruel discrimination against
human beings on account of the color of their skin. I never could understand it. When I travelled over the Southern
States thirty-five years ago organizing the workers, oh, what
a desolate, unpromising situation it was! I made my appeal
to them wherever I went, to open their doors to the colored
workers upon equal terms with the white workers, but they
refused. Poor as most of them were, they still felt themselves
superior to the colored people.

It is one of the surest indications of their own ignorance
and their own inferiority (applause); but, of course, they are
not conscious of it. There is what they call a race prejudice,
that is simply another name for ignorance (applause), and
you can trace it to that and that alone. It is comparatively easy
to forgive a man who has wronged you, but it is a very diffi-
cult thing to forgive the man that you have wronged. And this
is the attitude in which we find our colored brother who has
been the victim of this so-called civilization during the last
two centuries; and if there is any man who has read the history of the institution of chattel slavery on American soil, from
its beginning—from its inception 7through all of its frightful
stages, and who does not blush for himself and for his Anglo-
Saxon race, it is because he is something less than a real human being. (Applause.)

Stolen from their native land, torn from their families ruth-
lessly by the brutal hand of conquest, and then thrown
aboard vessels and herded like animals, half of them perish-
ing on the way over from starvation or disease or ill-treat-
ment, and the rest put upon auction blocks and sold to the
highest or lowest bidders, and then through the years that

followed designedly kept in ignorance and then despised, persecuted and punished because of their alleged inferiority!

The colored man has just as much in him that is potential and capable of development as the white man (great applause); and all he needs is a chance, that is all; he has never had that chance. (Renewed applause.)

I am sometimes surprised to think of the claims that are made in the name of religion and the much-vaunted Christian civilization that has everything in it but Christianity. (Applause.) Even in the great Christian Church the colored people have got to sit aloft—(A Voice: "Next to Heaven." Laughter.)—and I have had many a heated argument down in the Southern States and sometimes narrowly avoided trouble, making the contention that the colored man was a human being and had some rights that the white man ought to respect. (Applause.)

I remember on one occasion down in Atlanta, we had a Labor meeting and they had a loft to which the colored people were admitted. It was so far aloft that I could hardly see them (laughter) and I wondered if they could hear me; but they did, because their ears were attuned to a voice that had some promise for them. (Applause.) And I noted in the course of my address that I received no applause from below; it all came from the loft. (Laughter.) I paused long enough to say "the intelligence of this audience is in the gallery" 8(laughter and applause); and if they had had intelligence enough to understand what I said, I might have been lynched that night. (Laughter.)

On another occasion down at Montgomery, Alabama, where I was to speak at the Opera House, they had the line sharply drawn and said no colored people should be admitted. It so happened that the colored people had worked most faithfully and energetically for the success of that meeting, and when they appointed a committee which came to my hotel and notified me that they were to be excluded, I said, "We will go there together, and if you are excluded, so will I be excluded; if you cannot be admitted, I will not speak." (Great applause.) Well, there is one thing that the "superior" white man loves better than he hates the Negro, and that is the coin. (Laughter.) The manager had $50 coming for the use of the Opera House, and he wanted the money, and when I said I wouldn't speak unless he opened the doors to the colored people, he changed his mind very reluctantly to receive his $50. (Applause.)

When we were organizing the American Railway Union in 1893, I stood on the floor of that Convention all through its deliberations appealing to the delegates to open the door to admit the colored as well as the white man upon equal terms. They refused, and then came a strike and they expected the colored porters and waiters to stand by them. If they had only admitted these porters and waiters to membership in the American Railway Union there would have been a different story of that strike, for it would certainly have had a different result.

I remember one occasion down in Louisville, Kentucky, where we were organizing and they refused to admit colored workers to the union. A strike followed—a strike ordered exclusively by the white workers. After having ignored the colored workers and refused them admission, the strike came and the colored workers walked out with the white ones. Notwithstanding 9they had been excluded and insulted, they went out, and the strike had not lasted long until the white men went back to work and broke the strike, leaving the colored men out in the cold in spite of their loyalty to the white workers.

I have a word to you workers—you colored workers—about your duty in this campaign—your duty to yourselves, your families, your class and to humanity. I am not here asking for anything for myself. If I were seeking office, you know, I would not be in the Socialist Party. (Applause and laughter.) I want to speak to you very plainly to-night, especially you colored people, and have you understand that it is not in my power to do anything for you but to take my place side by side with you. That is all I can do. (Applause.) But while I can do nothing for you there is nothing that you cannot do for yourselves. (Applause.) There is one thing that I want to impress upon your minds to-night; it is self-respect. You can compel the respect of others only when you respect yourselves. (Applause.) As long as you are willing to be the menials and servants and slaves of the white people, that is what you will be. (Applause.) You have to realize that there are 12,000,000 of you in this nation, and that if you will unite and stand together and be true to each other, you will develop a power that will command respect. (Applause.) As long as you are unorganized—as long as you are indifferent, as long as you are satisfied to remain in ignorance you will invite contempt and receive it, but when you rise in the majesty of your manhood and womanhood, close up the ranks and stand together, you will command respect and consideration and you will receive it. (Thunderous applause.) It is the only way you ever will receive it. Everything depends upon your education. You have a brain; you can develop your capacity for clear-thinking. That is a duty owing to yourselves and your class, to your race and to humanity. (Applause.) That is the appeal I am making to you to-night.

10 Haven't you been long enough in the service of the capitalist parties to realize that they have no earthly use for you save only as they can perpetuate their system and keep you in servitude? The Republican party has trafficked in you, lo, these many years; the party that is unspeakably corrupt but still claims a monopoly of Abraham Lincoln and brazenly calls itself the party of Lincoln—what use have they for you? There was a time in my life, before I became a Socialist—when I was still young and had the vanity of youth and the ambition and enthusiasm of a boy—when I permitted myself as a member of the Democratic party to be elected to a State Legislature. I have been trying to live it down. (Laughter.) I am as much ashamed of that as I am proud of having gone to jail. (Applause and laughter.)

There is a peculiar fatality that seems to hang over me. Every time I am nominated as a candidate for President by the Socialists, the capitalists send me to jail or to the penitentiary. (Laughter.) Some paper said: "Debs started for the White House and got as far as Atlanta." (Laughter.)

I was, as I have said, a member of a Legislature. I used to meet with the politicians—Republicans as well as the Democrats; I became familiar with their political methods; I heard them over and over say in campaigning: "Now, we have got to figure on how to handle the "Nigger" vote; how much does it amount to and what will it take?" Well, a thousand colored voters are worth about one job on the police force or a mail carrier; if there are only about 500, why, a spittoon-cleaning job at the courthouse. That is about all they have ever given you and all they ever will give you. They do not associate with you; they have nothing in common with you. They want you segregated. When a race riot of any description comes, they are always armed against you. You know what they have done for you in the last thirty years in the way of recognizing you decently as human beings and giving 11you an equal chance with other human beings to work out your destiny.

Now, if you still persist—you colored people—in remaining in either the Republican or the Democratic party, you are stultifying yourselves; you are insulting your race; you are barring the door in your own faces—the door that leads to emancipation. The time has come for you to realize what your position is in these capitalist parties. They are both alike. I challenge anybody anywhere to show me the slightest difference between them from the working man's point of view.

I am speaking for the workers to-night. It does not make any difference to me where they were born or what the color of their skin may be, or what their religion is, or their creed, or anything of that kind. I ask no question as to that; they are all of the working class, the lower class, the class that does all of society's useful work, that produces all its wealth, and makes all the sacrifices of health and limb and life through all the hours of the day and night; the class without which the whole social fabric would collapse in an instant. It is this class regardless of color that creates and supports all civilization; this class that in all the ages of the past, throughout history, in every nation on earth has been the lower class; for the badge of Labor has always been the symbol of servitude and upon the brow of Labor there has always been the brand of social inferiority.

In the ancient world your ancestors were slaves, owned by their masters, whipped by their masters, put to death by their masters the same as other domestic animals. In the Middle Ages for a thousand years the serfs were not allowed to own an inch of soil; they could work only on condition that they produced for the benefit of the idle, aristocratic lord and baron who owned the land and who rioted in the luxury wrung from their sweat and misery. They also fought for 12him to enlarge his domain believing in their ignorance it was their patriotic duty to fight and die for the sovereign baron who looked down upon them with contempt. You are no longer the slave or the serf, but you are the wage earner in the present capitalist system. Your interests are all identical; you do all the useful, productive work but you do not work for yourselves; you have no legal right to work; you can work only if you are permitted to work by the owners of the tools with which you work. You made the tools and use the tools; but they own them and they might almost as well own you; for as long as you work with their tools, what you produce belongs to them; they become fabulously rich producing nothing while you remain poor producing everything. And this applies to white and black alike.

The race question as we come to understand it, resolves itself into a class question. At bottom it is a class question. The capitalist cares no more about the white worker than about the black worker. What he wants is labor power—cheap labor power; he does not care whether it is wrapped up in a white skin or a black skin.

Has he one bit more consideration for the white slave than he has for the black slave? No, not at all; they are all the same to him regardless of color; they are all in the working class; they are his legitimate prey. He owns the natural resources; he owns the tools; they have got to produce for him.

Under chattel slavery, the colored man seized with the aspiration to be free, ran away from his master. You do not run away from yours; when you run it is not away from but toward the factory whistle; you are afraid you won't get there soon enough. You work for your master and he becomes rich, and he does not know you; and why should he? He belongs to the upper class; you are in the lower class. He is useless and that is why he is in the upper class. (Laughter 13and applause.) Parasites all go to the top; they all float on the surface.

But now comes an election! That is the season of the year when their politicians come before you white and black workers. They do not discriminate against you colored people then. On the contrary they are glad to look into your intelligent faces and tell you that the beads of honest sweat that glisten on your manly brow are more precious than the jewels that blaze and flash in the coronet of a queen. (Laughter.) That is the one kind of jewelry—the one monopoly you absolutely control. They tell you that they are so greatly impressed by your intelligence and so proud to stand in your presence. But after the election is over they fold up their tents and like the Arab, they silently fade away. They do not associate with you; you do not belong to the same clubs they do. You do not play golf with them on their links; you don't wear

11

the same kind of clothes they do nor live in the same houses, nor eat the same kind of food. No; they are in a class of their own, notwithstanding you are all supposed to be absolutely equal before the law.

This is capitalism under which an insignificant minority of our people own and control the Nation's industries—all the sources and means of our common life. They would if they could own the sunlight and have a meter on every sunbeam. They have taken possession of about everything else. You are at their mercy. When you work it is by their consent; when you work it is for them; when you work it is primarily to produce profit for them; not to enable you to support your wife and children; that is purely incidental.

Under this system you workers white and black are scarcely above the animal plane. You work and produce like the silkworm; like the coral insect that builds islands and continents and perishes as it builds; and when you die you leave no trace behind that you were ever upon earth.

14You are not hired to think but to work. That is why they call you "hands." You will hear them say: "I work a hundred hands"; I work fifty "Niggers." Black "hands"; white "hands"; all "hands" (laughter); not men, but "hands." The capitalist calls you his "hands"; he himself is not a hand; he is a head; he lives in a palace and you are his "hands"; and the "hands" vote on election day to perpetuate the system under which he is the head and they are the hands; in which he is at the top and they at the bottom; and that is why the "hands" are told that this is the greatest country on the face of the earth—the one country in which all enjoy equal liberty.

The time has come for you to open your eyes and to stand erect and to realize that you have a head as well as hands; that you can think as well as work; and if you will but unite and think and act in accordance with your intelligence, you need no longer to deform your hands in the interest of the parasites that hold you in contempt. They are an insignificant minority and yet they rule in every department of this Government, and they rule through your ignorance, and the Socialist is frank enough to tell you that you are ignorant that you may become intelligent.

We do not flatter you and call you intelligent to keep you ignorant. We would have you understand that your masters rule because of your ignorance, because you still insist upon remaining in the Republican party or the Democratic party—and they are equally corrupt, only more so; both are financed from the same source, and our Comrade Chairman quite aptly quoted Sinclair, the oil king, in confessing to the United States Senate Committee investigating his deals that he contributes to both Republican and Democratic campaign funds. And why should he not? They are both his parties; both stand for his system; for the private ownership of this nation's industries; for the exploitation of the working class; for wage-slavery, and 15if that is what you want, stay with them; they will fulfill that program to your heart's content.

But have you not within you the holy spark of freedom, the glowing aspiration to be a man?—**not a slave but a MAN!** You must know what that is—a being with a soul that throbs with a desire and aspiration to know life. The working class do not know life. They are absorbed in maintaining an existence and that is not life; and while they are engaged in the endless struggle that taxes their energies, devitalizes and ages them prematurely, wears them out and casts them on the scrap-heap, they are not living. They are not permitted to know what life is in its larger, nobler and diviner meaning. They are never thrilled with those higher and holier emotions that put them in touch with all that lifts up and elevates men and women until they can, from the loftiest altitudes, sing to the stars. They do not know what music is. And the capitalists themselves are not very much better off. How wholly undeveloped they are in that higher intellectual, moral and spiritual sense! I have met many of them. I have been amazed at their ignorance. They are shrewd, to be sure; they are cunning; they can instinctively see an opening for profit; oh, they have a marvellous faculty for seeing a chance to skin somebody, and especially each other. (Laughter.) They belong to the same church; they go to the same prayer meeting but when they approach the edge of a "business" transaction, oh, how keenly they eye each other; not because they do not know each other, but because they do. Each is a good Christian and each is trying to avoid just what he is trying to do to the other. (Applause.)

Take them just as you find them; put them on this stand tonight; ask them a few questions about the history of their own country and you will be appalled by their ignorance. Point out to them a magnificent painting on canvas that breathes and throbs with genius; they have little or no capacity for its appreciation. Point out to them a great plumed monarch of 16the forest; the kind you can put your arms about it and hear its mighty heart throb; the kind that dominates the forest by its majesty and inspired Joyce Kilmer's beautiful poetic homage. You remember Joyce Kilmer—put to death, murdered in the late war; one of the fine poetic souls slaughtered and sacrificed on the altar of Mammon. It was he who wrote: "A tree that in the spring may wear, a nest of robins in its hair. Poems are made by fools like me, but only God can make a tree!" And you point out that towering and venerable tree to the fully developed capitalist and he regards it soberly for a moment and then draws forth his lead pencil and figures out how many feet of commercial lumber there are in that proposition. (Laughter.)

I wish I had time enough—but I have not—to trace American history from the days of the Revolution when the "Fathers" made their monumental mistake by compromising with chattel slavery. Had they but taken the advice of Thomas Paine (applause) the Civil War would not have resulted; that terrible sacrifice would have been averted. Thomas Paine protested and wrote the first article ever written in this country against chattel slavery just as he wrote the first article ever written in this country in favor of woman's rights—the same heroic Thomas Paine whose religious beliefs in "The Age of Reason" that followed completely isolated him from all intelligent understanding, from all human sympathy, and he is not yet forgiven for having had the courage to be true to himself and to the best he knew.

Thomas Paine inspired the Declaration of Independence that Thomas Jefferson wrote. (Applause.)

You call Washington to-day the "father of his country." And yet in his day he was denounced as a "notorious outlaw." (Applause.) The "father of his country" was the owner of chattel slaves as were the rest of the "fathers." They thought that perfectly 17consistent with that period; it does not detract from their historic achievement.

I can understand why the Tory press—the press of the then ruling class—charged Washington with being a common thief for confiscating their property. He was literally despised by them when he unsheathed his sword to fight for independence.

Thomas Jefferson was denounced as a vicious incendiary, Sam Adams as a disreputable agitator and Patrick Henry—you know what they said of him. (Applause.) I stood not long ago upon the spot where he stood when he hurled his immortal challenge in the face of the Government and exclaimed: "Give me liberty or give me death"; and I fancied I heard the hisses of the aristocrats that thronged the gallery who despised and denounced him as a traitor to his country. What was the state of his country at that time? A great majority of the colonists in their ignorance believed that God had anointed a king from on high to rule over them, and to question the divine authority of that king was treason, and he who was guilty must be punished without mercy. That was the blind stupidity of the great majority. Here let it be observed that the minorities have made the history of this world. The popular and reactionary majorities have perished in oblivion in their own ignorance.

In every age there have been a few men and women with new ideas—ideas in conflict with the established order of things. The class in power have always insisted upon perpetuating that power; they want no change; they combat every idea that suggests a change; they want to feel secure in "the established order of things."

In every age there have been a few men and women with moral courage, who stood erect and defied the storms of hatred and detraction. After a time—after they had been persecuted, vilified and imprisoned—after they had been burned at the stake and their 18ashes scattered to the winds by the hands of hate—the slow-moving world finally caught up to where they stood and fought for humanity and then it paused long enough to weave garlands for their graves and erect monuments where they sleep.

There were only a few of the American revolutionary leaders; only a few; and they stood face to face with a gainsaying populace who protested: "We believe in the king and we must be loyal to the king." They did not believe that the people had capacity for self-government; they were too weak, too helpless and dependent, and God had to provide them with a king to rule over them. That is what they believed. There were only a few who said: "We do not need a king; we can govern ourselves"; and they persisted in their odious agitation until they finally aroused the colonists and then came the war and the king was overthrown; the divine right to rule was trampled under foot with contempt; the foundations of the Republic were laid; the immortal Declaration was issued, and for the first time in history, politically speaking, men stood forth clothed to a limited extent with sovereignty.

How many of you are aware of the fact that the first drop of blood shed in that revolutionary struggle was that of a Negro? Crispus Attucks, to whom Boston has now erected a monument, was the first to be shot down by the British soldiers in the Boston massacre. (Applause.) And he was a Negro—the man whose blood was first to be shed for American independence; but you do not read that in the school histories. (Applause.) The Negro gets no credit for that martyrdom.

If there is any institution in the history of the world, the recollection of which should turn the cheek of humanity crimson with shame, it is the infamous institution of chattel slavery in the United States. (Applause.) There is no parallel to it in sheer, stark brutality in all the history of the world. You have 19never been given the facts; you never will be by the standard historians—they who represent the interests of the ruling class who subsidize and support them. You will never get that history until it is written by the working class itself. And some day it will be written. Some time American history will be reviewed. You never hear much about the people in history. You read about the exploits of the murderous military chieftains. All history glorifies them, but about the common people—the people who alone make history, how little reference is made to them! McMaster made a departure in his history and for the first time you now read about the lives of the common people in American history. Hitherto their achievements have not been deemed of sufficient importance to place upon record.

We come down to the final development of the institution of chattel slavery which culminated in the terrible war. The great majority, of course, upheld that brutal institution. And likewise the politicians and statesmen (so-called), the editors and the preachers—oh, how many there were who solemnly opened their Bibles and quoted passages to show that slavery had been ordained of God himself and that it was wicked to oppose it! Of the few heroic souls who declared it a crime Elijah Lovejoy was one of the first, and appealed to me in my earliest boyhood. I think I can almost hear him even now;

"I have sworn eternal opposition to slavery and by the help of God, I will not turn back." And then they murdered him! Garrison followed and then Wendell Phillips (applause); and the great towering, commanding intellectual and moral figure in that fierce struggle was Wendell Phillips. (Applause.) He saw it most clearly of all, faced it most courageously of all, and never once faltered in his devotion to the colored race. (Applause.) After chattel slavery had been abolished Garrison believed that the struggle was over—but he was mistaken—Wendell Phillips knew better, and some estrangement resulted on that account.

20Wendell Phillips, with discerning and prophetic vision, said: "This is the prelude—just the prelude to the far greater struggle—the struggle that will involve not only the black slaves but all the slaves of the earth in the mighty movement for their common emancipation." That is what Wendell Phillips said and he wrote the first Socialist platform ever written in the United States. Read the platform he wrote as far back as 1871 and see how uncompromisingly he faced the situation. They threatened him with the vengeance of the mob but he did not falter, he never wavered.

Wendell Phillips was a most wonderful combination of head and heart, soul and conscience (applause), and when the real truth is known about his commanding part in that historic struggle, the colored people will know that the real champion they had from first to last was Wendell Philips. (Great applause.)

I am not unmindful of the heroic part that William Lloyd Garrison took, or Theodore Parker, or Gerrit Smith who was driven insane by their brutal persecution; or Susan B. Anthony or Elizabeth Cady Stanton or Maria Childs, or any of those magnificent women who were in the forefront espousing the cause of their sex and at the same time the cause of the disfranchised Negro; who faced insult and persecution through many years. I have them all in mind and from my heart I pay the humble tribute of my gratitude and my admiration and love to them all.

But the greatest hero of them all was John Brown. (Thunderous applause.) I have taken time enough to go to Charlestown and to Harper's Ferry, and I have walked in his footsteps all the way from the old engine house where he made his heroic stand until he gave up his noble life on the gallows—every step of the way. And I thought of his wondrous courage and consecration and of the majesty, the spiritual loftiness of a human being who could give up his life as freely as he did for a lowly and despised race that could not understand 21him. There were members of that race so subservient to the masters in their ignorance that they begged for the privilege of braining him while he was in prison; but they only excited his compassion because he knew it was due to the very institution of chattel slavery that they had been sunk to that bestial moral state.

John Brown, when the crisis came, stood forth almost alone and struck the blow—the immortal blow that put an end to that most infamous of human institutions. Victor Hugo from across the Atlantic protested: "Think of a republic murdering a liberator," when they were about to put him to death; and after they had executed him for his heroism and his humanitarianism, Victor Hugo said: "The time will come when you Americans will realize that your John Brown was a greater liberator than your George Washington." (Applause.)

I appreciate all these heroes and martyrs, including Lincoln, who was vilified as no other American statesman ever was by that cruel and relentless power that organized the Ku Klux Klan after the war, and which is now seeking to revive that fanatical institution for the persecution of the Negro.

I am on the colored man's side as against all those that are attempting to keep him in servitude. (Applause.) And I am glad that the colored people are exercising self-restraint and facing this persecution with intelligence, which is commanding more and more respect. Let the Ku Klux spend its force. It consists of the self-appointed custodians of American liberty; but just let them alone; give them time and they will soon enough complete their round and close up their record. (Applause.)

I honor and appreciate all those who stood forth through the revolutionary conflict—through the struggle against chattel slavery—all who served and sacrificed to make it possible for me to stand on this platform 22to-night and to enjoy some degree of liberty and progress. I thank them all, and the only way I can repay them is by doing, as they did for me, what I can for those who are to come after us. And that is why I am here to-night.

I want to make my modest contribution to this campaign

of education and organization that gives you the opportunity to register your protest against capitalist corruption and mis-rule as well as the degree of your class consciousness and intelligence. (Applause.)

A matter of local interest to you in this campaign is the housing proposition. The law expires in February coming. It will not be re-enacted by the old parties. All the combined landlords have launched a campaign of opposition to it. This is an issue in which the workers are especially concerned. The rich are not worried about housing conditions. It is the workers who will be the prey of the greedy landlords of New York. That is an important issue in this campaign and the Socialist Party stands squarely for the re-enactment of the housing law and for the curbing of capitalistic greed in the interest of better housing conditions for the benefit of the working class and the exploited and suffering poor. (Applause.)

There is another matter of local interest. I was waited on to-day at my hotel by a delegation of policemen and City firemen. When officers of the law call on me they usually have a warrant (laughter); but on this occasion they were on a perfectly friendly mission.

When we had our meeting at Brooklyn the other night they had half the police force of that section there, just as they had at Toledo, the police surrounding the Opera House. But Socialist meetings are uniformly orderly. (Applause.) You never hear of a disorderly Socialist meeting. We appeal to the intelligence of the people (applause); we seek to educate them. A Socialist meeting has something of a religious spirit in it.

23But they sent the police force there because they said "he is a very dangerous man; there is no telling what may happen when he comes to town." (Laughter.) You see they are afraid of a man who tells the truth (Applause); that is the one thing they cannot stand. (Applause.) And if you cannot be bribed or brow-beaten—if you cannot be intimidated, if you insist upon being true to your own soul's integrity, and speak what is in your heart, then of course, you must expect to pay the penalty, and I have been and am now ready to pay to the limit. I went down to Atlanta for three years almost; that was my fifth term in one of the peculiar educational institutions of capitalism and it has all had its good results. (Laughter.) But I have no bitterness; I have no resentment. I felt sorry for the man who had to lock me up. He did not want to do it.

Soon after I was in prison I came in touch with a colored man who had a most tragic history. He had been there for thirty years and ten years of that he had been placed in solitary confinement because they couldn't break his spirit. When they insulted him he resented it and defended himself. When I got down there I heard about him. His name was Sam Moore. He was one of the many, many colored men who never had a chance in life. In his childhood—in his very infancy he was tossed out into the world; he knew only poverty and neglect; his mother was dead seven years before he knew it. He was never in school; no one had ever given him a kind word; buffeted about he tried to help himself and fight his way along; he got arrested, as they all do, was put in jail, got into a quarrel and in a fight that followed he chanced to kill another prisoner when they sent him to the penitentiary, more than thirty years ago, and he has been there ever since. When I came in touch with him they said "he is a bad man." I soon found him to be a brother. The Chaplain was asked: "What has Debs done to Sam Moore, he is an entirely different man?" The Chaplain answered: 24"Just loves him; that's all." (Applause.) Oh, the magic and the power of human love, were it but understood! Sam Moore had never been touched by the hands of kindness; everything that was combative in his nature was developed by the cruel, inhuman treatment he had been subjected to all his life. And when I came down there and we met face to face on the same level, I said to myself, if I had been born as Sam Moore was and under the same condition, I would be Sam Moore; I would be where he is now. I am not one bit better than he. On the contrary I was reminded of the divine Easterner who prayed to his Allah: "Be Thou merciful to the vicious and forgive them; Thou hast already blessed the virtuous by making them so."

As I thought of Sam Moore and of the environment and conditions under which he had been reared and had to suffer and struggle, I made allowance accordingly, and he was the last inmate I saw when I left that prison.

There were almost three thousand human beings there. The prison is the poor man's institution; the rich don't go there, no matter what crime they may commit. About one-third of the prisoners were colored people, and they used to come to me when they had petitions to make or there was some little service I could render them. I used to write their letters and I could not but sympathize with them. They tried to segregate them in the prison. We were occasionally permitted to see moving pictures. They admitted the white men to one side of the auditorium and the colored men to the other side. Some of the white "superior" element said: "Let the Niggers sit in the rear"; and so on the next occasion they allowed the white men to occupy all the front seats and put the colored men in the rear where they could hardly see the stage. They appointed a committee to call on me to see what they could do about it. I said "I am with you; we will protest against the injustice." We did and we put an end 25to it. After that the colored men were given the same consideration as the white prisoners.

I loved all of those almost three thousand prisoners, charged with every conceivable offense against society. I treated them all as if they had been members of my own family, and there was not one of them I would not have invited to my table or to my home. They were poor, most of them ignorant; they never had a fair chance. They had, for the most part, committed some petty offense and were pushed into the penitentiary and branded as "convicts."

The lowest thing about a prison is often the prison guard—the only fellow I was ashamed to associate with. (Laughter.) The last inmate I saw when I left prison was Sam Moore. There was a fine woman in that neighborhood whose sympathy had been enlisted, and on the day I left she brought a beautiful cake she had baked. She said: "This is for Sam," and the warden said: "I will send it to him"; I said: "No; please send for Sam, I wish to place it in his hands and bid him good-bye." Sam came. There was something of the majesty of the man about him, notwithstanding his thirty years of cruel usage and persecution. He was like some monarch of the forest that the tempest had riven and denuded. But he still stood erect, unbroken in spirit. I presented him with the cake and the tears rolled down his face. At parting we put our arms around each other and wept together. That was my farewell scene in the Atlanta prison. I can still hear, in broken words, the sobbing entreaty: "I want to get out of here and to be where I can do for you and your family anything in my power all the rest of my life." That was Sam Moore, the man they had said was a desperado, an incorrigible and dangerous criminal. He was as tender and responsive as a child; the divine within him had not been extinguished; all he needed was the touch of human kindness; and that is what has been denied him and his race through all the centuries.

26Give a colored man the same chance, the same opportunity that you give a white man, and he will register as high upon the mental and moral thermometer of civilization. (Great applause.) Give him a chance! and that is what the Socialist Party is going to do. (Applause.) We admit colored members to our Party upon equal terms with the rest. We sit side by side with them in our Party councils. They are welcomed gladly to all our conferences and conventions. We treat them in no patronizing sense. We are not doing them any favor. They are our comrades and our equals, and we want them to have every right and privilege we enjoy.

I wish to speak a final word for the policemen and firemen. When they came to see me to-day and stated their mission, I declared myself in favor of their referendum. It is with this referendum they propose to establish a wage minimum of $2,500. The policemen and firemen are in the working class—all of them; and we are with them in their efforts to secure a living wage. (Applause.) You sometimes think these policemen, when they seek to "protect society against the Socialists," are hostile to us. When we were at Brooklyn, as I passed through their serried ranks they whispered to me: "We are with you." (Applause.) One of them said: "It will not do for the Ku Klux to try to do anything to you here to-night." (Laughter.) They are trying to get $2,500 a year and they are entitled to it; considering the cost of living $2,500 with a family to support is a small enough income. We are with them and we hope you will all join in their effort to secure a living wage for themselves and their families. (Applause.)

I want to say a word for the "Messenger" and to commend the high ability of its editorial management. I read it with especial pride and satisfaction. It is a high grade publication. It is a true champion of the colored workers and every one of you ought to give it your encouragement and support.

27I appeal directly to you colored workers. You have got to build up your own press; you have got to develop your own power; you will never count until you do. Unite with all other workers in the unions; unite with them in the Socialist Party; develop your industrial power and your political power. Most of you are inclined to buy the capitalist newspapers and support the capitalist press and every time there is a strike you know what side they are on. You will never hear the truth until you hear it through your own press.

Then there is the daily "Leader," a Labor paper published in New York. The "Leader" ought to have the support of the workers. We have got to build up a press of our own. It is vitally important because everything depends upon education.

It is a tremendous struggle. It is going to take time and what most people call sacrifice. There is no sacrifice, however, so far as I am concerned, because what I can give the cause I give with joy and it comes back to me in riches untold. I have made no sacrifice for Socialism. I would sacrifice only if I refused the privilege of serving it. I would sacrifice only if I violated my conscience and failed to give myself to this struggle with every atom of my energy and every drop of my blood. And with what joy! It keeps me young and vigorous and alive in action. It is a privilege and not a sacrifice to go to jail for the cause. (Applause.) How gladly I would spend the rest of my days there if need be, or go to the gallows, or anywhere in the service of Socialism! (Great applause.)

You and I and all of us are alike interested in the present campaign. You hear the same "argument" on the part of the old politicians you have heard here in New York for over forty years. I am not personally interested in their vilification of each other—their mutual charges and accusations. Take their word for it and they are all grafters and thieves. They say so and they certainly know each other for they have been 28in close affiliation for a long time. If you are going to cast your vote for either of these corrupt capitalist parties and if you are going to give your support to those candidates who are committed to keep you in servitude how can you look yourselves in the face on the day following election without a blush of shame?

Sever your relations with these capitalist parties that are of the past. They disgrace the memory of Jefferson and Lincoln. Sever your relations with them and join this new party, this party of the future, especially you young people. It is vain to appeal to some of the older ones; they are petrified; they have long since ceased to think; they are led; they belong to the Republican party because their father did, or to the Democratic party because their grandfather did. Everything since their grandfather lived has changed except their grandsons. (Laughter.) If you have the spirit of the future; if you have the aspirations to be men and women; if you are capable of thinking for yourselves, stand up for just once and see how long a shadow you can cast in the sunlight; take an inventory of your mental and moral resources and ask yourselves in sober earnest: "What can we do for ourselves, and for our class, and for humanity"? Think!! You have never done that in the past. You have the capacity to see, to think, to understand, and to take your place in this great modern crusade, the greatest in all history.

Everywhere the awakening workers are lifting their bowed bodies from the earth—these toiling and producing masses who have been the mudsills of society through all the ages past. They are learning at last how to stand erect and hold up their heads and press forward toward the dawn, keeping step to the inspiring heart throbs of the impending Social revolution. They are of all races; they are of all colors, all creeds, all nationalities. They have made a great beginning in Russia. (Applause.) The Soviet Republic has stood for five years against the combined capitalisms 29of the world; vilified and misrepresented shamefully, but they still hold the fort. The reason we do not recognize their Republic is because for the first time in history they have set up a Government of the working class; and if that experiment succeeds, good-bye to capitalism throughout the world! (Applause.) That is why our capitalist Government does not recognize Soviet Russia. We were not too proud to recognize the Czar nor to have intercourse with Russia whilst Siberia was in existence and human beings were treated like wild beasts; when women were put under the lash and sent to Siberia and brutalized and dehumanized. We could calmly contemplate all this and our President could send congratulations on his birthday to the imperial Czar of Russia. We could then have perfect intercourse with that Government, but we are now so sensitive under our present high standard of moral ethics that we cannot recognize Soviet Russia. But the time will come when the United States will recognize the Soviet Republic of the Russian people.

Meanwhile we will wait, watch and work. We will improve our minds and develop our capacity to think and act together. We shall get closer and closer in touch day by day, increasing

the store of our knowledge, dispelling the darkness of ignorance, and moving steadily toward the light.

You and I and all of us are comrades; we are brothers and
sisters. Let us get into perfect unity with each other and stand
upon one common basis of equality with the high aspiration to emancipate ourselves from the degrading thraldoms
of past ages. Let us as workers organize industrially so that
we may be fitted to take control of all industry. We will then
relieve the Rockefellers, the Garys and the Sinclairs of their
sinecure jobs; we will give them an opportunity to make an
honest living for the first time in their lives. (Applause.) We
will take full possession of industry. Every man and woman
will have the inalienable 30right to work with the most im-
proved machinery. The machine will be the only slave—no
body to starve, no back to scar, no heart to break, no soul to
crush. The machine will work for us and we shall then have
leisure time enough to cultivate the graces of life; to know
and love and serve each other, and to begin the march to the
first real civilization the world has ever known. The liberat-
ing hour is soon to strike—and if you are true to yourselves
you can speed the day of its coming. Triumphant Internation-
al Socialism will then proclaim the emancipation of the working class and the brotherhood of all mankind. At last that inspiring vision of Ingersoll will have been realized:

"I can see a world where thrones have crumbled and where
kings are dust. The aristocracy of idleness has perished from
the earth. I can see a world without a slave; man at last is free.
Nature's forces have by science been enslaved. Lightning and
light, wind and wave, frost and flame and all the secret, sub-
tle forces of earth and air are the tireless toilers for the human race. I can see a world at peace, adorned with every form
of art, with music's myriad voices thrilled while lips are rich
with words of love and truth. A world in which no exile sighs,
no prisoner mourns—upon which the shadow of the cruel gallows no longer falls. I can see a world where Labor reaps its
full reward and work and worth go hand in hand. I can see
a race without disease of flesh or brain, shapely and fair, the
married harmony of form and function, and as I look, life
lengthens, joy deepens, love canopies the earth, while over all
in the great dome there shines the eternal star of hope."

And in that crowning hour men and women can walk the
highlands side by side and enjoy the enrapturing vision of a

land without a master, a land without a slave; a land radiant and resplendent in the perfect triumph of the brotherhood of all mankind.

And now from my heart I thank you for the patience 31and the kindly interest with which you have listened to me. I thank you for having been here to-night and for giving me the privilege of appearing upon the platform with these comrades that I know you are going to stand by on Tuesday next—Comrade Lucille Randolph, your candidate, whom I would be so proud to vote for it if I could, and Comrade Ollendorff, who incarnate the true spirit, the high principles and the lofty ideals of the Socialist movement. They are your candidates and my candidates, and if you are true to them as they have been to you, they will be triumphantly elected next week. And now good-night and a thousand thanks and good wishes! (Great and prolonged applause.)

Edited by A. Philip Randolph and Chandler

www.ingramcontent.com/pod-product-compliance
Lightning Source LLC
Chambersburg PA
CBHW021344290326
41933CB00037B/726